Referencing the Bible's Gospel Stories According to Mathew, Luke and John.

This Gospel storybook belongs to:

Name
Date

Traveling to Bethlehem

A Story of the First Christmas

Retold by
Pam Blake-Virostko

Edited by Donna Watson • *Illustrated by Marcia Mattingly Reller*

This book is sincerely dedicated to Our Lord
Whose divine mission touched my heart to help
Teach our children about Jesus.

-Pamela Blake-Virostko

CrossBooks™
A Division of LifeWay
1663 Liberty Drive
Bloomington, IN 47403
www.crossbooks.com
Phone: 1-866-879-0502

With special thanks to:
Anita Gambill, Children's Choir Director
Songs performed by: Makayla Clutter, Kaylie Gambill,
Michaela Gambill, Christopher Kaufman,
Lydia May, Loretta Peffers, Ariel Poff and Yzabel Tio

Music Arrangements by Donna Watson
CD produced by Andrew Snowden, Snowden Music Services

Audio storybook with songs available at www.MusicalGospelForKids.com

First published by CrossBooks 9/28/2010

ISBN: 978-1-6150-7334-4 (sc)

Printed in the United States of America

This book is printed on acid-free paper.

CROSS
BOOKS

Traveling to Bethlehem

A Story of the First Christmas

Christmas is a special time with trees and gifts and fun.
The very first Christmas time, God gave to us His Son.
So now we'll tell the story of how Christmas came to be.
We remember the birth of Jesus and the first nativity.

God our father loves us so, He chose to be a man
By sending to the earth His son to bring to us His plan.
God sent the Angel Gabriel to the land of Galilee,
For Mary had been chosen, let's go there, listen and see…

Mary was alone in prayer before she went to bed.
When suddenly the angel came and greeted her and said,
"Rejoice Mary! You are blessed, and there is none like you."
But, frightened, Mary answered back, "What are you going to do?"
"Don't be afraid," the angel said. "I've not come to bring you harm.
God sent me here to speak to you". So Mary listened without alarm.

He said, "Your God has chosen you. Among women there is no other.
You will give birth to a baby boy. You will become a mother.
You will call Him Jesus. He will be God's only Son.
He will be King forever to rule the chosen ones."

"But I'm not married," Mary said, "I've not been with a man.
How could I have a baby? I just don't understand."

Nothing is impossible for our great God to do!
So Gabriel said, "The Holy Spirit will overshadow you."
Mary said, "I love my God. I'll serve Him in every way.
I say **Yes** for He is good. Let it be done as you say."

Mary's Song

Mary, you're going to be a mommy!
Mary, you're going to have a son!
Mary, you'll call Him baby Jesus.
Mary, you're the chosen one.

Mary, do not be frightened,
Just because you've never known a man.
God in heaven will be His Father,
By the power of the Spirit,
And the wave of His hand.

Mary, you're going to be a mommy!
Mary, you're going to have a son!

Joseph was the man that Mary promised she would wed.
A righteous, holy man and only good of him was said.
He was from the line of David who long ago was King.
Joseph never wanted shame upon his family to bring.

So when he found that Mary already was with child
To say he was upset is putting it quite mild.
He paced inside his room and cried, "Whatever should I do?
I can't believe this happened. Mary promised to be true.
The baby is not mine, I know. There is nothing I can say.
This isn't right. She has to go. There'll be no wedding day!"

But Joseph trusted in his God. And you know he loved Him too.
God sent an angel to his dreams to tell him what to do.
"Joseph, son of David, do not fear what God has done.
Take Mary for your wife for she will bear <u>His</u> only son.
You will call him Jesus and to man he'll be the Savior".
And when the angel said these things she disappeared like vapor!

Morning came and Joseph woke. He stood and rubbed his eyes.
He recalled his dream, "God spoke to me!", Joseph realized.
"I will do as the angel said. I'll take Mary into my home.
And I'll care for the baby Jesus as though he were my very own."

Joseph's Dream

Joseph, it is ok.
Trust in God to show you the way.

Christ Child Jesus, soon to be born,
Means God is with us, the Savior and Lord.

You can take Mary to be your wife,
Love her and care for her all of your life.

Joseph, it is ok.
Trust in God to show you the way.

In a distant country to the East the stars were studied by Wise Men.
The Wise Men knew that a special star meant a miracle soon would happen.
The star meant God would be born on earth to become a mighty king.
They could follow the star! It would lead them to this wondrous, amazing thing.

One night as the Wise Men studied the skies the new star did appear.
They were so excited to see it! They knew the time was near.
So they gathered to them their precious gifts of frankincense, myrrh and gold.
They packed their bags and left their home to see this sight to behold.

Three Wise Men Traveling Afar

Three Wise Men, traveling afar, following a star, not knowing where they're going.
Little King, where will you be born? How can we find you? Look into the sky, beautiful star.
Wonder where they're going, wonder how far. Jesus, where will you be born? How can we find you?

The Wise Men traveled following the star, their journey was almost done,
When they met King Herod, an evil king, who feared the birth of God's Son.
The Wise Men arrived in Jerusalem and went before Herod's throne.
They asked, "Where is the baby, King of the Jews? Tell us where he will be born."

Now Herod was not very happy when he heard the Wise Men's news.
"What do you mean", he grumbled, "I'm the King of the Jews!"

For Herod had no intention of letting another King reign.
He decided to fool the Wise Men and thought of an evil plan.

"Hmmm…" Herod sneered as he rubbed his chin, His voice was mean and gritty.
Then he asked his High Priest, "Where will this take place? Tell me in which city!"

The High Priest unrolled the scriptures, carefully so not to be torn.

"It is written, Bethlehem of Judea is where the Savior will be born".

So Herod told the Wise Men, "Now, I'll tell you what you should do ... when you find him, come back and tell me, so that I can "*worship*" him too".

"Thank you, King Herod," the Wise Men said. "We will do just as you say".

Then they left to travel to Bethlehem, and continued on their way.

Now the ruler of all the land at that time was named Caesar Augustus.
He wanted to count all the people he ruled, so he ordered what was called a census.
Each person had to be counted in the town their family was from.
Joseph's line was the Family of David, and his town was Bethlehem.

The distance to travel from Nazareth, where Joseph and Mary called home,
Was 70 miles, a great distance, and they had to travel alone.
They walked or rode on a donkey for in those days there were no cars.
Mary's baby was due to be born any day. How hard to travel that far!

Traveling To Bethlehem

Traveling to Bethlehem, no place to call home.
Traveling to Bethlehem, where Jesus will be born.

The road is a long painful quest.
A troubled path ... in need of rest.
But with faith and hope they are strong.
Their joy is coming and it won't be long!

Traveling to Bethlehem, don't know where they'll stay.
Traveling to Bethlehem, trusting God to show the way!

It was late when Mary and Joseph arrived and Mary said, "We're almost there!"
But the town was so full of people, there was no place to stay anywhere.

Joseph and Mary went to each inn to find a room with a bed.
"Go away!" they were told, "There's no room for you here!",
Was all that they heard instead.
Finally, quite late, at the edge of the town, Joseph gave one final plea.
"Please sir", he said, "We must have a room. My wife is expecting a baby!"

The innkeeper said, "I do not have a room, but I'll tell you what I can do.
There's a barn with fresh straw in the stable. I can offer that to you."
"Yes, thank you so much", Joseph sighed with relief.
"I was getting so very worried."
Then Mary said, "Joseph, the baby, it's soon! I think we better hurry!"

That very night she gave birth to her
son and Jesus' life did begin.

There in a stable where animals lived,
for there was no room at the inn.

Mary wrapped baby Jesus in cloths to keep
warm and since he had no bed,

She laid him to sleep in a manger of hay,
where the animals all were fed.

He Came To Us In The Night Time

He came to us in the nighttime, while most were still asleep.
He came to be our Savior, a gift for us to keep.

The love flowing from God's heart, the touch from His strong hand.
Gave to us in the nighttime, Himself made into man.

He came to us in the nighttime, so fragile and so weak.
A birth of hope for sinners, the path for all who seek.

A candle in the darkness, the flame for all to see
Came to us in the nighttime, this future king to be.

In the fields outside of Bethlehem shepherds kept flocks of sheep.
They stayed up all night to watch out for danger, they watched and did not sleep.
Well on the night that Jesus was born the angels in heaven were singing.
It was to those lowly shepherds God's good news the angels were bringing.

The shepherds were watching over their sheep, what a beautiful peaceful night.
When the angel appeared to tell about Jesus, the shepherds got such a fright!

"Don't be afraid", the angel said. "I'm bringing good news of great joy.
It's for you and for all of the world to hear – the birth of a baby boy.
In Bethlehem, David's city, a savior has been born.
He is the blessed Messiah. He is the Holy Lord.
Let this be a sign so that you can see this amazing and wonderful thing.
Wrapped in cloths, asleep in a manger, you'll find the newborn King!"

The shepherds were so excited, they hurried to Bethlehem to see.
They found Jesus just as the angel had said, and worshiped on bended knee.

There appeared many heavenly angels, near and far you could hear them sing.
"Joy to the world. The Lord has come! Let earth receive her king."

The song filled the earth and the heavens bringing praises again and again.
"Glory to God in the highest, peace on earth and good will toward men."

So that was the very first Christmas. Jesus came and God's plan had begun.
It was the day that God gave to us His only begotten Son.

The End

Musical Gospel For Kids

Did you enjoy this story about the first Christmas? Be sure to read Volume 2 of the Musical Gospel for Kids series, *Growing Up In Wisdom*. Find out what happens next to Joseph, Mary and Jesus. Do the Wise Men return to Jerusalem to tell King Herod where the baby Jesus is? Where does Jesus grow up? What are some of the things that happen to Jesus when he was a baby and a young boy?

The six new original songs in *Growing Up In Wisdom* will touch your heart. The storybook and songs bring a message of learning and understanding from the Gospel stories of Jesus as a baby and a little boy.

Traveling to Bethlehem: A Story of the First Christmas
Audio Storybook With Songs Available Online!

Go to www.MusicalGospelForKids.com to listen for FREE!

You may purchase the complete storybook audio download from the web site … or order the digitally mastered CD. Plus review the latest news and products that are available from **Musical Gospel For Kids.**

Sheet music for the original songs is available for choir, piano and full orchestra. Look for our director's notes for performing a Christmas Play. You may contact:

Musical Gospel For Kids
c/o Pam Blake-Virostko
7546 S. Virostko Rd.
Rockville, IN 47872

Bringing the Bible's Gospel stories of Jesus Christ alive with poetry, drama, music and illustrations.

Wonderful for home, travel, bible study, church, plays and gifts.

Editing and Music Arrangements by Donna Watson, who has served in lay leadership as a worship leader, music director, Sunday school teacher, Bible Study leader and speaker. An active composer and music arranger, author of: *"Soundings – Finding the Depth of Your Faith in the Channels of Life"* – You can reach her at: www.MusicLady@indy.rr.com.

Artwork by Marcia Mattingly Reller, an illustrator and graphic designer working in Indianapolis, IN.

You can reach her at mreller1@att.net

Study Guide – Questions

1. What happened on the very first Christmas?
2. What is another name for the birth of Jesus?
3. Who is Jesus' mother?
4. Who did God send to talk to Mary to announce His intention for her?
5. Who is Jesus' real Father?
6. Who was Mary engaged to be married?
7. What was the Family Name that Joseph belonged to?
8. What did Joseph decide to do when he found out that Mary was expecting a baby before they were married?
9. What made Joseph change his mind about Mary and if he should marry her or not?
10. Did Joseph and Mary get married?
11. How did the Wise Men from the Far East know something amazing was going to happen on earth?
12. What was the amazing thing that the Wise Men knew was going to happen?
13. How could the Wise Men go to see the amazing thing?
14. What were the 3 precious gifts that the Wise Men were taking as gifts to give to Jesus?
15. Why did the Wise Men stop in Jerusalem on their way to find Jesus?
16. Who did the Wise Men ask, when they were in Jerusalem?
17. Was King Herod happy when he heard that the Savior was going to be born?
18. How did King Herod know the town where the Savior would be born?
19. Where did King Herod tell the Wise Men they could find Jesus?
20. What did King Herod tell the Wise Men they should do after they found Jesus?
21. Was King Herod telling the truth or was he lying when he said he wanted to find Jesus to worship him too?
22. Who was the ruler of all the land at the time of Jesus' birth?
23. What did Caesar Augustus order to happen at the time of Jesus' birth?
24. Where did Joseph and Mary live at this time?
25. Where did Joseph and Mary have to travel to be counted for the census?
26. How did Joseph and Mary get to Bethlehem?
27. Did Joseph and Mary get to Bethlehem early or late?
28. What did Joseph and Mary find when they arrived in Bethlehem?
29. What kind of place was Jesus born in?
30. What was Jesus' first bed when he was born?
31. Who were the very first visitors who got to see the newborn baby Jesus?
32. How did the shepherds know where to find Jesus?
33. Who else appeared the night Jesus was born and what were they doing?
34. Who is God's only begotten Son?

(Answers on next page)

Study Guide – Answers

1. Jesus was born.
2. The Nativity.
3. Mary.
4. The Angel Gabriel.
5. God.
6. Joseph.
7. The Family of David.
8. He decided to not get married to Mary.
9. God sent an angel to speak to him in his dream.
10. Yes.
11. A certain bright star would appear in the sky.
12. God would be born on earth to become a mighty king.
13. They could follow the star because it would lead them.
14. Frankincense, myrrh and gold.
15. To ask in which town they could find the newborn king.
16. King Herod, who was king of the Jews.
17. No! He was angry because he did not want a new king to be born.
18. It was written in their Sacred Scriptures and the High Priest read it to him.
19. In Bethlehem of Judea.
20. Come back and tell him exactly where Jesus is.
21. Herod was lying when he said he wanted to worship Jesus.
22. Caesar Augustus.
23. A census of all the land at that time.
24. Nazareth.
25. To Bethlehem.
26. They walked or rode on a donkey.
27. Late.
28. All of the places to stay were full. There was no room for them anywhere.
29. A stable where animals lived.
30. A manager of hay where animals were fed.
31. The shepherds from the fields outside of Bethlehem.
32. An angel of the Lord appeared and told them about Jesus.
33. Many angels appeared and they were singing and praising God.
34. Jesus.

God Bless You and your family!

Pam Blake-Virostko

Author Pam Blake-Virostko is a wife, mother, grandmother, mandolin musician, and songwriter. She spent eleven years leading her church's guitar group and teaching children songs and choreography. *Traveling to Bethlehem* has evolved into its present format from a skit that she wrote for her church's Christmas Eve service. Her hopes are to continue writing children's Gospel stories in this same format.